the
BLACK TRANSMAN
& TRANSWOMAN

AWARENESS * EQUALITY* ADVOCACY* EMPOWERMENT* PIONEERS in HISTORY

lulu books
presents

THE
BLACK
TRANSMAN
&TRANSWOMAN

AWARENESS EQUALITY ADVOCACY EMPOWERMENT PIONEER's in HISTORY

tesa de'Carlo

the
BLACK TRANSMAN
& TRANSWOMAN

AWARENESS * EQUALITY* ADVOCACY* EMPOWERMENT* PIONEERS in HISTORY

tess deCarlo

www.lulu.com
2019

Cover design by tess de'Carlo

First Printing: 2018

ISBN 978-0-359-41957-9

www.LULU.com
Lulu Press
860 Aviation Parkway,
Suite 300
Morrisville, NC 27560

tessdecarlo@aol.com

copyright provisions

under the

17 US Code § 107 – Limitations on exclusive rights. Fair Use.

Notwithstanding the provisions of sections 106 and 106A, the fair use of a copyrighted work, including such use by reproduction in copies or photo-records or by any other means specified by that section, for purposes such as criticism, comment, news reporting, teaching (including multiple copies for classroom use), scholarship, or research, is not an infringement of copyright. In determining whether the use made of a work in any particular case is a fair use the factors to be considered shall include—

(1) the purpose and character of the use, including whether such use is of a commercial nature
or is for nonprofit educational purposes;

(2) the nature of the copyrighted work;

(3) the amount and substantiality of the portion used in relation to the copyrighted work as a whole; and

(4) the effect of the use upon the potential market for or value of the copyrighted work.

Dedication

To
the BLACK TRANSGENDER INDIVIDUAL's

who have persevered

to overcome

societies injustice, prejudice, bigotry, diversity

and have shown

empowerment in the development

for Trans Rights

and have put their name

in being PIONEERS in BLACK TRANS HISTORY

"And the day came when the risk to remain tight in a bud

was more painful

than the risk it took to blossom."

Anais Nin

CONTENTs

"A significant exploration of
'Who's Who'
within the
Historical Development
of Black Transgender History.

For additional information
please visit the world wide web,
Google, Wikipedia, Independents! !"

Foreword

What is transsexualism?

- Some estimate suggest that as many as 1 in 4,500 males may be transsexual

  •

  - and 1 in 8,000 females

  •

- Transsexualism is most commonly defined as the desire to live as the opposite sex accompanied by a wish to change the body to that preferred sex through surgery or hormone therapy

  •

The term was coined in the middle of the 20th Century, but there are many references to the phenomenon throughout history - from Ancient Greek mythology to Roman times

  •

- Anthropologists have found instances of transsexualism in most societies and cultures, including Native American tribes such as the Navajo who have words in their own language for transsexual men and women

Preface

To preserve historical prosperity,

words such as 'crossdresser','fagot'

"drag", 'faierie', hermaphrodite', transvestite', and 'tranny'

in additionally 'sex-change' and other like-terms

are used within their original content to indicate the vocabulary

terms indicative of the historical-philological semantics .

They are not intended to offend anyone.

The views and opinions expressed

are not necessarily those of the staff or management

of lulu publications,

nor the author,

nor of the Gatekeepers.

Introduction

An observation of the black transgender movement through history,

bringing attention to the wide variety of resources

and research used to such a marginalized group.

Heavily relying on archival, alchemy, resources,

examples of the author's own personal exploration and collection,

as well as the holdings (transcribed interviews, photographs, journals,
private letters, etc. contents of the world wide web.)

of the transgender Historical findings.

Also included are reproductions from photographic collections

held at major universities

and the archived psychiatric/medical records of patients who have had sex
change operations.

From the Gatekeepers to the modern day transgender experiences.

As educational as it may be perceived –

the sole purpose of this book is historical entertainment.

PIONEERS
in
BLACK TRANSGENDER HISTORY

AJITA WILSON

1950 ~ 1987

Ajita Wilson was a transsexual actress with an international cult following for her work in foreign films, started out as an entertainer in the red-light district of New York. Wilson had sex reassignment surgery in the mid-1970s. After the operation she started appearing in adult films in New York. Then she was discovered by a European hardcore film producer who got her roles in various French and Italian films of hardcore nature.

She would later become a JET Beauty of the Week, appearing in the magazine's 1981 August 20th issue. Her status as a transgender woman was not acknowledged until after her death in 1987..

In 1987 Wilson was in an automobile accident and died of a brain hemorrhage.

Ajita Wilson

tess deCarlo

ALEXANDER 'BEAR' GOODRUM

1960 ~ 2002

Alexander "Bear" Goodrum was a Black disabled,

bisexual transgender man, activist, and orator. Though known as an LGBTQIA+ rights activist, particularly advocating for trans and gender nonconforming civil liberties, Goodrum also worked in each of these marginalized communities.

Beginning his work in 1980, Goodrum was originally from Chicago, but made several moves to San Francisco and Tucson working as an activist for LGBTQIA+ and social justice rights. Once in Tucson, Goodrum created, founded, and directed the TGNet Arizona, a grassroots transgender advocacy and resource center. He was also a board member of the Tucson GLBT Commission and the Funding Exchange's OUT Fund, which provides grants (one of which is named after Goodrum) to LGBTQIA+ community organizing projects. Goodrum made himself well known within the Arizona LGBTQ advocacy community and was instrumental in creating meaningful change for LGBTQ individuals in Arizona.

In 1999, Goodrum was able to include his work on gender identity for a non-discrimination law. He is also well known for his groundbreaking work with the Arizona Transgender Workplace Project, an educational workshop for employers to foster inclusive and safe working environments and understand the needs, challenges, and rights of transgender and gender non-conforming employees and applicants.

Goodrum published a number of papers and articles and is widely known for Gender Identity 101: A Transgender Primer, which is still published on the Southern Arizona Gender Alliance's website. In September 2002, Goodrum died by suicide in a psychiatric hospital in Tucson.

Bear Goodrum was aware of the need to have an intersectional approach to social justice issues. We must follow his lead in creating inclusive spaces for trans and gender nonconforming folks, people with disabilities, and LGBQIA+ members in order to ensure the liberation of everyone.

tess deCarlo

ANDREA JENKINS

B ~ 1961

Andrea Jenkins is an American policy aide, politician, writer, performance artist, poet, and transgender activist.

She is known for being the first African-American openly transgender woman elected to public office in the United States, serving since January 2018 on the Minneapolis City Council.

tess deCarlo

The BLACK TRANSMEN & TRANSWOMEN PIONEERs in

ALTHEA GARRISON

October 7th, 1940

ALTHEA GARRISON is the first transgender
person to be elected to a state legislature (1992) in the United States'

Althea Garrison is an American politician from Boston, Massachusetts, who was elected as a Republican to the Massachusetts House of Representatives in 1992 and served one term from 1993 to 1995. Both before and after Garrison's successful bid for office, she has run unsuccessfully in multiple elections for the state legislature and Boston City Council as a Republican, Democrat or independent, which has resulted in her being described in the media as a "perennial candidate" Garrison is also known as the first transgender or transsexual person to be elected to a state legislature in the United States

Garrison was formerly known by the name A. C. Garson. Born in Hahira, Georgia. Garrison attended Hahira High School there. Garrison moved to Boston to attend beauty school, but went on to enroll in Newbury Junior College and received an associate degree there. Garrison later received a B.S. degree in administration from Suffolk University, an M.S. degree in management from Lesley College, an a certificate in special studies in administration and management from Harvard University.

According to records in the Suffolk County Probate Court, Garrison petitioned for a name change from A. C. Garson to Althea Garrison in 1976. The petition stated that the name Althea Garrison "is consistent with petitioner's appearance and medical condition and is the name by which 'he' will be known in the future.

In 1982 and 1986, Garrison ran unsuccessfully for the Massachusetts House of Representatives as a Democrat. She ran unsuccessfully for Boston City Council in 1983, 1985, 1987, 1989, and 1991. During the 1991 campaign, the Boston Herald noted that she had run for office nine times, although Garrison herself later described the race as her 10th or 11th bid for office. In the 1991 race, Garrison finished in third place in the District 7 preliminary election.

In 1992, Garrison ran successfully for the 5th Suffolk district in the Massachusetts House, representing the Dorchester and Roxbury areas of Boston. Garrison's 1992 election to the legislature was made possible in part by the fact that she challenged some of the signatures that the then-incumbent representative, Nelson Merced, had submitted to qualify for the Democratic primary ballot. Her challenge was successful and meant that Garrison did not have to run against an incumbent in the general election. In the general election, Garrison defeated Democratic candidate Irene Roman, 2,451 votes to 2,014.

The fact that Garrison had been formerly known as a male was not widely publicized until shortly after she was elected to the legislature. When the Boston Herald asked whether she was a man, Garrison denied it and ended the conversation when asked about her past, including her name change.

In the Massachusetts House, Garrison consistently voted in favor of labor unions, resulting in her being endorsed for re-election by the Massachusetts AFL-CIO and eight unions. On many votes, she voted with the Democrats in the legislature rather than with the Republicans. However, she opposed same-sex marriage and abortion.

Garrison was defeated in her 1994 bid for re-election by Democratic candidate Charlotte Golar Richie by a margin of 2,108 votes to 1,718

tess deCarlo

CARL MADGETT

Minister Carl Madgett, Activist

TransSaints Mid-West Regional Minister

Received the 2013 BTMI Advocacy honorable award is in recognition of individuals,groups and organizations who are dedicated to social change and are focused on equality,advocacy and empowerment. This is an ongoing award available to all throughout the year within your local community and annual awards recognitions are featured at each Black T.I.E.S. Annual Awards

tess deCarlo

CARTER BROWN

CARTER BROWN, Founder and Executive Director of Black Transmen, Inc. We are the first national, non-profit, Black trans led organization that empowers the Black Trans community through social advocacy, positive visibility, and building strong leadership. It was my personal experiences of having lack of support, resources, community, and equality as a Black transman that compelled me to create the organization.

Since we were founded in 2011, we have multiplied our presence and our impact on not only the Black Trans community, but much of society at large also. We work in alliance with several other leading organizations, schools, churches, medical providers, and media outlets, with the intent of establishing Black Transmen Inc. to be the indispensable resource for many issues facing the transgender community.

Currently Brown actively leds a host of over 35 board, staff and volunteer members of the organization, and is in the process of building state chapters in over 9 U.S. States, pioneering others by example to "Become The Change You Want To See In The World".

tess deCarlo

CeCe McDONALD

B ~ 1989

CeCe McDonald an African American bi trans woman and LGBTQ activist.

She came to national attention in June 2012 for accepting a plea bargain of 41 months for second-degree manslaughter of a man she stabbed after McDonald and her friends were assaulted in Minneapolis outside a bar near closing time. The attack, a year prior, was widely seen as racist and transphobic, and became physical when McDonald was struck in the face by the man's friend with "an alcoholic drink" glass causing a bleeding gash that needed stitches.

When McDonald was getting away from the bar the man came after her, she took a pair of scissors out of her purse and turned around to face him, he was stabbed in the chest and died from the wound. McDonald said she saw how her case was progressing so took the plea bargain rather than face trial and risk a possible 20-year term.

According to the *Bay Area Reporter* her conviction

"sparked outrage, and was viewed by many as an act of transphobia and racism against a woman who defended herself."

Although a woman, McDonald was housed in two men's prisons.

An online petition

"led to the state department of corrections administering
the full regimen of hormones she needed."

McDonald was released in January 2014 after serving 19 months.

CRYSTAL LEBEIJA

? ~ 1982

CRYSTAL LEBEIJA worked and competed on the Manhattan drag circuit and was crowned Miss Manhattan. At the time, she was one of only a few African American drag queens to be awarded a "Queen of the Ball" title at a drag ball organized by whites. In the 1960s and 1970s, drag queens of color were expected to whiten their appearance to help their chances at winning competitions and they often faced racist environments.

During the 1967 Miss All-America Camp Beauty Pageant held in New York City Towns Hall, LaBeija was upset with the bias and racism of the balls, as shown in the 1969 film "The Queen", when LaBeija, Miss Manhattan at the time, accuses the hostess of rigging the process for a white queen Rachel Harlow, formerly Miss Philadelphia. Shortly after, Labeija's friend, Lottie, convinces her to host a ball for black queens, the first to be hosted by a "House." The event was titled "Crystal

& Lottie LaBeija presents the first annual House of Labeija Ball at Up the Downstairs Case on West 115th Street & 5th Avenue in Harlem, NY.

Crystal LeBeija

tess deCarlo

ISIS KING

B ~ October 1st, 1985

Isis King is an American model, actress, and fashion designer. She was a contestant on both the eleventh cycle and the seventeenth cycle of the reality television show America's Next Top Model. She was the first trans woman to compete on the show, and became one of the most visible transgender people on television

JANET MOCK

B ~ March 10th, 1983

ANET MOCK's book *Redefining Realness:
My Path to Womanhood, Identity, Love & So Much More*

s a memoir and the debut book by Janet Mock , an American writer and
ransgender activist.

It was published on 1 February 2014 by Atria Books.

The book debuted in 19th position on *The New York Times*
Best Seller list for Hardcover Nonfiction.

Janet Mock with husband Aaron Tredwell

JONATHAN THUNDERWORD

Jonathon Thunderword is a theologian, a scholar, and a free thinker. He is an omni-faith, multi-spiritual practitioner who is a part of Mata Amritanandamayi Center.

He is an ordained minister, founder of Finding Another Right Road Authentically and Holistically (FARRAH) and founder of By the Way Ministry in Virginia.

He is also affiliated with National Alliance on Mental Illness (NAMI) Faith Network, Pacific School of Religion (alumnus), Lehrhaus Judaica (Hebrew student), Black Trans Men International, and Brothers Rising (Oakland, CA).

KYE ALLUMS

B ~ October 23rd, 1989 ~

KYE ALLUMS is a former college basketball player at for the George Washington Colonials women's basketball team of George Washing University (GWU) and a transgender pioneer.

He is now a transgender advocate, public speaker, artist, and mentor to LGBT youth. In 2010, Allums, a trans man, became the first openly transgender NCAA Division 1 college athlete.

Allums graduated from Centennial high School in Circle Pines, Minnesota,. He played three seasons as a guard on the women's team at GWU. In May 2011, it was reported that Allums had decided to leave the GWU basketball team.

Allums now has his own website, www.kyeallums.com, where people can stay updated about his life.

KYLAR BROADUS

Kylar Broadus, founder of the Trans People of Color Coalition (TPOCC) became the first trans person ever to testify before the US Senate. Broadus's testimony was in support of the Employment Non-Discrimination Act, or ENDA.

In the early 1990s, Broadus worked for a major financial institution, although he didn't disclose its name during the hearing. After announcing in 1995 he would undergo gender transitioning, Broadus said he was forced out of his role. Broadus said:

"At work, when I decided to actually transition,
I had been there for a number of years,
and I'm a workaholic,
and it was disheartening to me
that all this could be pulled out from under me
because people weren't comfortable with the person that I am,"

w/Laverne Cox   w/President Barack Obama   Kylar

His written testimony details receiving harassing phone calls, receiving assignments after hours that were due early next morning and being forbidden from talking to certain people.

Broadus recalls,

"I still sit here today with almost tears in my eyes,
It's devastating,
it's demoralizing and dehumanizing to be put in that position."

tess deCarlo

LADY CHABLIS

March 11th, 1957 ~ September 8th, 2016

Brenda Dale Knox transgender woman, known professionally as The Lady Chablis, was an American actress, author 'Hiding My Candy', and drag performer. Through exposure in the bestselling nonfiction book *Midnight in the Garden of Good and Evil* that reads like fiction, and its 1997 film adaptation, she became one of the first drag performers to be accepted by a wider audience

Chablis frequently performed at her "home" nightclub of Club One in Savannah Georgia, where she was known as the "Grand Empress". Chablis traveled the US performing at various venues and special events, such as gay pride gatherings. She also appeared on radio shows. She was a prominent character in John Berendt's best-selling book *Midnight in the Garden of Good and Evil*, (1994), and played herself in the 1997 film adaptation, starring Kevin Spacey and John Cusack and directed by Clint Eastwood.

The Lady Chablis was featured in the closing segment of the Savannah episode of Bizarre Foods America on The Travel Channel.

She joined host Andrew Zimmern at several Savannah restaurants including Elizabeth on 37th. In 2012, she was interviewed inSavannah, Georgia on the local television and internet talk show "MAMA Knows Best Talk Show" season 2 episode 1. On April 19, 2013 Chablis performed for the grand opening of Mama's Cabaret in Lewiston, Maine with "MAMA" Savannah Georgia.

Lady Chablis opposite actor John Cusack

(scene from "Midnight in the Garden of Good and Evil')

LAVERNE COX

Laverne Cox, American actress and LGBTQIA+ activist, is the First Transgender Person to appear on the Cover of *Time Magazine*. May 29, 2014.

LADONVITO LOPEZ

LaDONVITO LOPEZ,

American writer "Thoughts through Transition".

LOUIS 'L.J.' MITCHELL

Rev. Louis Mitchell is a pioneering "intentional man". Known around the country and abroad as an elder, advocate, teacher, student, minister, parent and friend. He serves as the Co-founder and Executive Director of Transfaith™/Interfaith Working Group and as the Associate Minister of South Congregational Church in Springfield, MA.

Rev. Mitchell is a proud father to his daughter, Kahlo, and co-parent with her mother, Krysia L. Villon. Louis has been in recovery for over three decades and been involved in the fight for health, respect and self-determination since the early 1980s, with deep engagement in political, mental health, recovery, and church contexts.

He brings his own learned experiences, a broad range of resources, theories and studies, to offer a fresh, "on the ground", open-hearted, holistic strategy to the work of individual and community healing, intersectional diversity planning and commitment to personal and community agency and solvency.

LUCY HICKS ANDERSON

1886 ~ 1954

Lucy Hicks Anderson

was born Tobias Lawson in Waddy, Kentucky, in 1886.
From a very early age Anderson was adamant that she was not male,
identifying as female in a time period before the term transgender existed.
After going to doctors and being told to just let Lucy live as a young

woman, Lucy's parents decided to side with physicians, and she began wearing dresses to school and being known as Lucy.

In 1945 she was arrested and tried for perjury,
under the justification that she had lied about her sex on her marriage license and was impersonating a woman

tess deCarlo

LUCY HICKS ANDERSON

MARCELLE COOK-DANIELS

1960 ~ 2000

tess deCarlo

Marcelle Cook-Daniels had two traits that set him apart from many other Black trans leaders.

The first and most important trait is that he didn't think of the world in the categories so many of us now organize our lives around. He was able to see and support individuals beyond their demographic labels, yes, but he also understood that individuals often lead lives that are intimately involved with others who may "belong to different categories." Some of this viewpoint came from his own interracial partnership, where class similarities and world outlook far outweighed the racial differences. His personal relationship was also where he learned to greatly value the type of partnerships in which people worked together for a single purpose, using each partner's strengths to bolster and fill in the other partner's strengths; he and his partner Loree Cook-Daniels were proud of their ability to set joint goals and then play different roles in order to reach them.

That was the approach they took when the first, 1995 and 1996, FTM conferences divided trans people from their partners, restricting partners from many workshops and offering vastly different agendas (including some that were offensively stereotypical, such as scheduling "shopping") to non-trans partners. Having had over a decade of being treated as equal partners in a lesbian couple, the sudden experience of having people tell them they were now different and unequal was jarring and unacceptable to both Marcelle and Loree.

Luckily, an opportunity to create a different path soon came. Gary Bowen, an American Indian transman who had founded American Boyz on the East Coast, agreed that the best and fastest way to advance the trans community was to include SOFFAs – the newly-coined term for Significant Others, Friends, Family and Allies. He also expressed a strong interest in having an FTM conference on the East Coast, since both the previous conferences had been on the West Coast. Despite now living on the West Coast themselves, Marcelle and Loree saw the new conference – which Gary Bowen named True Spirit, partly in honor of his Native heritage – as an opportunity to establish an inclusive approach to organizing for the trans community. They lobbied hard for Gary to expand his vision to a national conference, sweetening the deal by offering Loree as an unpaid, half-time staffer (supported, obviously, by Marcelle) in exchange for the expansion. Gary agreed, and Loree and Gary spent the next several years working closely together from across the country (a possibility that had only recently emerged as the result of the internet) to build both the True Spirit conferences (held annually from 1997 to 2002) and American Boyz itself.

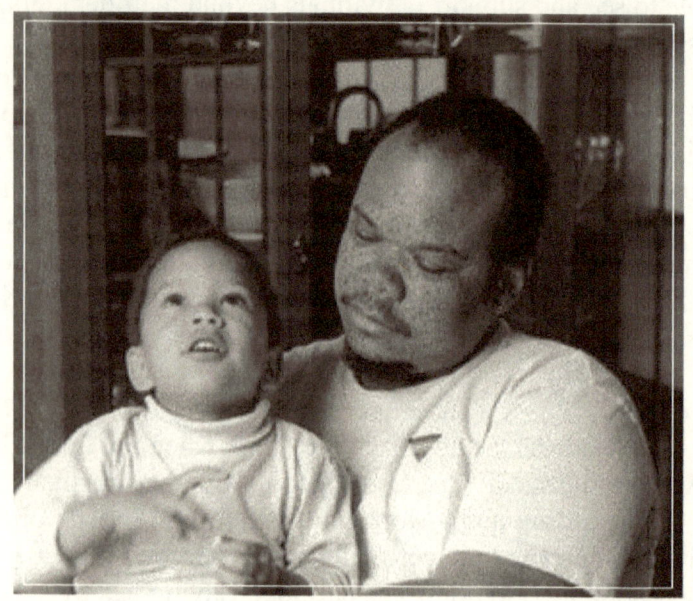

Marcelle, in addition to bankrolling one of AmBoyz/True Spirit's key staffers (Gary continued to finance himself), stepped into other roles as needed. At least once, he provided the credit card guarantee the conference hotel required, served as Security Director and Treasurer (which at that point was a high-stakes job, since many conference registrations were paid in cash), and took on miscellaneous other, mostly-behind-the-scenes, tasks as needed. He was immensely proud of the conferences: they provided a model in which all members of the community felt equally welcomed, and yet where differences were acknowledged and met: practically every demographic group, including people with disabilities and Arab-Americans, had their own liaison, many of whom developed identity-specific resource lists. The conferences also all had at least one person of color chair or co-chair the conference, once

Gary gave up that role. This is remarkable in part because it wasn't explicitly planned; it was only in retrospect that anyone noticed that aspect of the leadership.

Of course, it wasn't all rosy. Marcelle took a lot of pushback from other people of color when he opposed a proposal to waive all conference fees for people of color. He felt that it was unfair and an exercise in stereotyping to change the existing policy of providing scholarships for those people – of any race – who were low-income and could not afford the conference fee. As a middle-class Black man who was helping underwrite the conference, the proposal also made him feel invisible. He also was challenged for not giving a speech in 2000, when Loree became the first partner to ever keynote a transgender conference. He was immensely proud of what he and Loree had together achieved by that speech, and devastated that others could not see that the keynote was for him — a background kind of guy who described himself as "the SOFFA's SOFFA" — as much his achievement as Loree's. These experiences, among others, made him feel unseen and unvalued for who he was as an individual, apart from his skin color and gender. They were part of what led to him taking his own life later in 2000.

tess deCarlo

MARSHA P. JOHNSON

August 24th, 1945
July 6th, 1992

Marsha P. Johnson
was an American gay liberation activist
and self-identified drag queen.
Known as an outspoken advocate for gay rights,
Johnson was one of the prominent figures
in the Stonewall uprising
of 1969

tess deCarlo

RITA HESTER

Rita Hester, November 30th, 1963 ~ November 28th, 1998

Rita Hester was a transgender African American woman who was murdered in Allston, Massachusetts on November 28, 1998.

She was murdered two days before her 35th birthday. On the evening of Nov. 28, 1998, police found the African-American transgender woman in her apartment, stabbed in the chest a staggering 20 times. She was somehow still alive but died from cardiac arrest as soon as she arrived at the hospital.

tess deCarlo

Rita Hester

SIR LADY JAVA

August 20th, 1943

Sir Lady Java
is an American transgender rights activist,
exotic dancer, singer, comedian, and actress.
Active on stage, television, radio and film
from the mid-1960s to around 1980,
she is a popular and influential personality in the Los Angeles-area
African-American LGBT community.
She challenged LA's anti-crossdressing law.

tess deCarlo

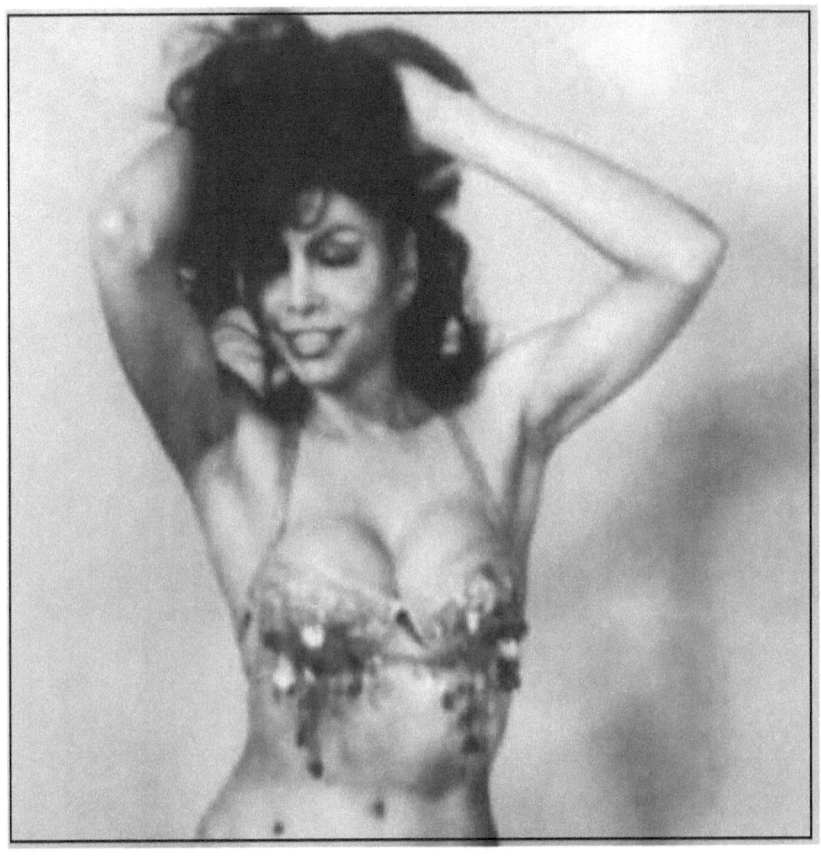

Sir Lady Java

TRACIE 'AFRICA' NORMAN

B ~ 1951

Tracey "Africa" Norman is an American model.
Norman was the first African-American transgender woman model to
appear on a box of Clairol hair-coloring in the 1970s. Originally from

Newark, New Jersey, Africa has modeled and been photographed for such publications as Essence, Vogue Italia and Harper's Bazaar India.

TRACY JADA O'BRIEN

May 1951 ~

TRACY JADA O'BRIEN

since surviving the mean streets of San Francisco's Tenderloin District in
the 1970s as a young transgender street kid,
she has become one of the most respected and elegant role models of the
transgender community — a testament to beauty, survival and
perseverance.
O'Brien is a certified addictions treatment counselor and spent six years as
a counselor and coordinator of extend services at Stepping Stone of San
Diego, a nationally renowned alcohol and drug treatment facility
specifically serving the GLBT community.

She is the FOUNDER of The TRACY JADA O'BRIEN TRANSGENDER
DAY OF EMPOWERMENT STUDENT SCHOLARSHIP FUND.

TRACY JADA O'BRIEN

tess deCarlo

WILMER 'LITTLE AXE' BROADNAX

December 28th, 1916 ~ June 1st, 1992

Willmer M. Broadnax also known as "Little Ax", "Wilbur", "Willie", and "Wilmer", was an American hard gospel quartet singer.

After moving to southern California in the mid-1940s, Wilmer and brother, William, joined the Southern Gospel Singers, a group which performed primarily on weekends. Wilmer and William soon formed their own quartet, the Golden Echoes. William eventually left for Atlanta, where he joined the Five Trumpets, but Willmer stayed on as lead singer. In 1949 the group recorded a single of "When the Saints Go Marching In" for Speciality Records.

In 1950, Broadnax joined the Spirit of Memphis Quartet. Along with Broadnax, the group featured two other leads – Jethro 'Jet' Bledsoe, a bluesy crooner, and Silas Steele, a baritone. The Spirit of Memphis Quartet recorded for King Records, and Broadnax appeared on their releases at least until 1952. Shortly after that, Broadnax moved on, working with The Fairfield Four, and in the early 1960s as one of the replacements for Archie Brownlee in the Five Blind Boys of Mississippi. Until 1965 Wilmer headed a quartet called "Little Ax and the Golden Echoes," which released some singles on Peacock Records. By then, quartet singing was fading in commercial viability, and Broadnax retired from touring.

In retirement, Broadnax continued to record new material occasionally with the Blind Boys into the 1970s and 1980s. Upon Broadnex's death in 1992, it was discovered that Broadnax was a trans man

Fairfield Four w/ Wilmer 'Little Axe' Broadnax (bottom row – right-hand)

tess deCarlo

References

Glossary

C.E.: Common Era. Synonymous with A.D. but without religious bias.

Censer:-A heat-proof container in which incense is burned. It is associated with the element air.

Ceremonial Magick:-A highly codified magickal tradition based upon Kabbala, the Jewish-Gnostic mystical teachings.

Chakras:-Seven major energy vortexes found in the human body. Each is usually associated with a color. They are: crown - white; third-eye - purple; throat - blue; chest - pink or green; navel - yellow; abdomen - orange; groin - red. Smaller vortexes are located in the hands and feet as well.

Chalice:-A ritual tool. It represents the female principals of creation.

Channeling:-A New Age practice wherein you allow a discarnate entity to "borrow" your body to speak to others either through automatic writing or verbally.

Chaplet:-A crown for the head usually made of flowers and worn at Beltane.

Charge:-The Originally written in modern form by Doreen Valiente, it is a story of the message from Goddess to Her children.

Charging:-To infuse an object with personal power.

Charms:-Either an amulet or talisman that has been charmed by saying an incantation over it and instilling it with energy for a specific task.

Circle:-Sacred space wherein all magick is to be worked and all ritual contained. It both holds ritual energy until the witch is ready to release it, and provides protection for the witch.

Cleansing:-Removing negative energies from an object or space.

Collective Unconsciousness:-Term used to describe the sentient connection of all living things, past and present. See also Akashic Records.

Coming of Age Ritual:-At age 13 for boys, and at the time of a girl's first menses, Pagan children are seen as spiritual adults. The ritual celebrates their new maturity. Generally this is the age when they are permitted membership in covens.

Cone of Power:-Psychic energy raised and focused by either an individual or group mind (coven) to achieve a definite purpose.

Conscious Mind:-The analytical, materially-based, rational half of our consciousness. The part of our mind that is at work while we balance our checkbooks, theorize, communicate, and perform other acts related to the physical world.

Consecration:-The act of blessing an object or place by instilling it with positive energy.

Coven:-A group of thirteen or fewer witches that work together in an organized fashion for positive magickal endeavors or to perform religious ceremonies.

Covenstead:-The meeting place of witches, often a fixed building or place where the witch can feel safe and at home.

Craft:-Witchcraft

Crone:-Aspect of the Goddess represented by the old woman. Symbolized by the waning moon, the carrion crow, the cauldron, the color black. Her Sabbats are Mabon and Samhain.

Cross-Quarter Days:-Refers to Sabbats not falling on the solstices or equinoxes.

Days of Power:-See Sabbat. They can also be days triggered by astrological occurrences - your birthday, a woman's menstrual cycle, your dedication/initiation anniversary.

Dedication:-The process where an individual accepts the Craft as their path and vows to study and learn all that is necessary to reach adept ship. It is a conscious preparation to accept something new into your life and stick with it, regardless of the highs and lows that may follow.

Deosil:-Clockwise, the direction in which the shadow on a sundial moves as the Sun "moves" across the sky. Deosil is symbolic of life, positive magick, positive energies.

Dirk:-Ritual knife of the Scottish tradition.

Divination:-The magickal art of using tools and symbols to gather information from the Collective Unconsciousness. This can be on people, places, things and events past, present, and future.

Divine Power:-The unmanifested, pure energy that exists within the Goddess and God. The life force, the ultimate source of all things.

Dowsing:-The divinatory art of using a pendulum or stick to find the actual location of a person, place, thing, or element.

Drawing Down the Moon: A ritual performed during the Full Moon by witches to empower themselves and unite their essence with a particular deity, usually the Goddess.

Drawing Down the Sun:-Lesser-known and lesser-used companion ritual to Drawing Down the Moon in which the essence of the Sun God is drawn into the body of a male witch.

Duality:-The opposite of polarity. When used as a religious term, it separates two opposites such as good and evil and places those characteristics into two completely separate God-forms.

Earth Magick:-The energy that exists within stones, herbs, flames, wind, and other natural objects.

Earth Plane:-Metaphor for your normal waking consciousness, or for the everyday, solid world we live in.

Elements:-Usually: Earth, air, fire, water. The building blocks of the universe. Everything that exists contains one or more of these energies. Some include a fifth element- spirit or Akasha.

Elementals:-Archetypical spirit beings associated with one of the four elements. Elementals are sometimes called Faeries.

Eleven-Secretive tradition of the craft which works closely with elemental beings.

Enchantment:-A magickal object that must be kept absolutely secret and hidden from all human eyes and affects a hidden aura. They must be charmed first. Gems and magickal writing are good items to use.

Eostre's Eggs:-Colored, decorated eggs of Ostara; named for the Teutonic Goddess Eostre.

Esbat:-A ritual usually occurring on the Full Moon and dedicated to the Goddess in her lunar aspect.

Evocation:-To call something out from within.

Faerie:-See Elemental

Faerie Burgh:-Mound of earth which covers a faerie colony's underground home.

Familiar:-An animal that has a spiritual bone with a witch; many times a family witch. Familiars can also be entities that dwell on the astral plane.

Fascination:-A mental effort to control another animal or person's mind. Also known as "mind-bending". Often considered unethical.

Folklore:-Traditional sayings, cures, faerie tales, and folk wisdom of a particular locale which is separate from their mythology.

Folk Magick:-The Practice of projecting personal power, as well as the energies within natural objects such as herbs, and crystals, to bring about needed changes.

Gaea/Gaia:-Mother Earth.

God:-Masculine aspect of deity.

Goddess:-Feminine aspect of deity.

rain Dolly:-Figure usually woven at Imbolc from dried sheaves of grain collected at the previous harvest. The dolly is traditionally burned at Yule and a new one made the following Imbolc.

Great Rite:-Symbolic sexual union (also sacred marriage) of the Goddess and God that is enacted at Beltane in many traditions, and other Sabbats in other traditions. It symbolizes the primal act of creation from which all life comes.

Green Man:-Another name for the God

Grimorie:-A magickal workbook containing ritual information, formulae, magickal properties of natural objects and preparation of ritual equipment. Often used interchangeably with Book of Shadows.

Grounding:-To disperse excess energy generated during magickal work by sending it into the earth. It also means the process of centering one's self in the physical world both before and after any ritual or astral experience.

Grove:-Synonymous with coven.

Guardians:-Ceremonial magicians use the Guardians of the Watchtowers or Four Quarters. Some witches use them, too.

Hand Fasting:-A Pagan wedding.

Herbalism:-Art of using herbs to facilitate human needs both magickally and medicinally.

Higher Self:-That part of us which connects our corporeal minds to the Collective Unconscious and with the divine knowledge of the universe.

Hiving Off:-This term is used for a small coven which splits off from a larger one. Sometimes this is done to keep the gatherings of a manageable size, other times covens split over philosophical differences.

Horned God:-One of the most prevalent God-images in Paganism. NOT Satan or the Devil!!!

Initiation:-A process whereby an individual is introduced or admitted into a coven. Usually a ritual occasion. Not to be confused with dedication.

Incense:-Ritual burning of herbs, oils, or other aromatic items to scent the air during acts of magick and ritual, and to better help the witch attune to the goal of the working.

Invocation:-To bring something in from without.

Jew-itch:-Name coined by some Pagans of Jewish origin who are actively seeking out the pagan roots of their birth religion.

Karma:-The belief that one's thoughts and deeds can either be counted against them or added to their spiritual path across several life times.

Kabbala:-Mystical teaching from the Jewish-Gnostic tradition. Ceremonial Magick and the Alexandrian traditions are based in these teachings. Also, Qabala.

Labrys:-A double-headed ax which symbolizes the Goddess in Her Lunar aspect. Has roots in ancient Crete.

Left-Hand Path:-Refers to the practice of using magick to control others, to change the will of others, for personal gain. Generally frowned upon by true Wiccans and Witch's. Dark Magick.

Libation:-Ritually given portion of food or drink to a deity, nature spirit, or ghost.

Macrocosm:-The world around us.

Magick:-The projection of natural energies (such as personal power) to being about needed change. Energy exists in all things: us, plants, stones, colors, sounds, movements, words. Magick is the process of raising this energy, giving it purpose, and releasing it. Magick is a natural, not supernatural, practice, but is little understood. Magick is neither black nor white. It simply is. What the magician decides to do with the magick is another matter...

Magick Circle:-A sphere constructed of personal power in which rituals are usually performed. Within it the witch is protected from outside forces. The sphere extends both above and below the surface of the ground.

Magickal System:-The basic set of guidelines relating to the worship of specific Gods and Goddesses or cultural traditions.

Male Mysteries:-Pagan study which attempts to reclaim the power and mystery of the old Gods for today's Pagan males.

Matrifocal:-Term used to denote pre-patriarchal life when family clans centered around and lived near or on clan matriarch.

May Pole:-Sexual symbol of Beltane representing the phallus.

Meditation:-Reflection, contemplation- turning inward toward the self, or outward toward Deity or nature. A quiet time in which the practitioner may either dwell upon particular thoughts or symbols, or allow them to come unbidden.

Megalith:-A huge stone monument or structure. Stonehenge is the best-known example of a megalith.

Menhir:-A huge stone probably erected by early peoples for religious, spiritual, or magickal reasons.

Microcosm:-The world within us.

Monotheism:-Belief in one supreme deity who has no other forms and/of displays no other aspects.

Mother:-The aspect of the Goddess representing motherhood, mid-life, and fertility. She is represented by the full moon, the egg, the colors red and green. Her Sabbats are Midsummer and Lughnasadh.

Myth:-Cycles Body of lore about any land or people that makes up their mythology.

New Age:-The mixing of metaphysical practices with a structured religion.

New Religion:-Pagan term used in reference to Christianity.

Nursery Rhyme:-Cute doggerel or poems supposedly written for the amusement of children. Much Pagan lore was hidden in these ditties during the years of witch persecutions.

Occult:-Literal meaning is "hidden" and is broadly applied to a wide range of metaphysical topics which lie outside the accepted realm of mainstream theologies.

Occultist:-One who practices and or studies a variety of occult subjects.

Ogham:-Celtic equivalent of the Teutonic runes. The ancient alphabet of the Celtic people.

Old Ones:-The A term which refers to all aspects of the Goddess and God.

Old Religion:-A name for Paganism as it pre-dates Christianity by at least 20,000 years.

Pagan/Neo-Pagan:-General term for followers of Wicca and other magickal, shamanistic, and polytheistic Earth-based religions. Also used to refer to pre-Christian religious and magickal systems.

Paganing:-When a baby is presented in circle to the Goddess and God, and given a craft name which s/he will keep until about 13 and can choose their own at their Coming of Age celebration.

Pantheon:-A collection or group of Gods and Goddesses in a particular religious or mythical structure.

Pantheism:-Belief in many deities who are really one because they are all merely aspects of the single creative life source. Paganism is pantheistic.

Passion Over Ritual:-Ritual observed when a loved one has dies.

PAST-LIFE REGRESSION:-Act of using meditation or guided meditation to pass through the veil of linear time and perceive experiences encountered in a previous existence.

Path Working:-Using astral projection, bi-location, or dream time to accomplish a specific goal. Also called vision questing.

Patriarchal:-Term used to apply to the world since the matrifocal clans that worshipped Goddesses were supplanted by codified religions that honor all-male deity(s).

Pendulum:-A divinatory device consisting of a string attached to a heavy object, such as a quartz crystal, root, or ring. The free end of the string is held in the hand, the elbows steadied against a flat surface, and a question is asked. The movement of the heavy object's swings determines the answer. It is a tool which contacts the psychic mind.

Pentacle:-A circle surrounding a five-pointed, upright star (pentagram). Worn as a symbol of a witch's beliefs. Many witches consider wearing it inverted to be blasphemy of their faith and is commonly associated with Satanism.

Pentagram:-The basic interlaces five-pointed star, visualized with one point up. It represents the five elements: Earth, Air, Fire, Water, and Spirit. It is a symbol of power and protection.

Personal Power:-The energy which sustains our bodies. It originates within the Goddess and God. We first absorb it from our biological mother within the womb, and later from food, water, the Moon and Sun, and other natural objects.

Polarity:-The concept of equal, opposite energies. The Eastern Yin Yang is a perfect example. Yin is cold; yang is hot. Other examples: Goddess/God, night/day, Moon/Sun, birth/death, dark/light, psychic mind/unconscious mind. Universal balance.

Polytheism:-Belief in the existence of many unrelated deities each with their own dominion and interests who have no spiritual or familial relationships to one another.

Poppets:-Anthropomorphic dolls used to represent certain human beings in magick spells.

Projective Hand:-The hand thought to be the point through which personal power is sent from the body. Normally the hand used for manual activities such as writing, dialing the phone, etc. It is also the hand in which tools such as the athame and wand are held.

Psychic Mind:-The subconscious, or unconscious mind, in which we receive psychic impressions. It is at work when we sleep, dream, and meditate. It is our direct link with the Divine, and with the larger, nonphysical world around us.

Psychism:-The act of being consciously psychic, in which the psychic mind and conscious mind are linked and working in harmony. Also known as psychic awareness.

Quabala:-See Kabbala

Receptive Hand:-The hand through which energy is received into the body. The left hand in right-handed persons, the reverse for left-handed persons.

Rede:-The Basic tenet of witchcraft. "An it harm none, do what thou will.

Reincarnation:-The process of repeated incarnations in human form to allow evolution of the sexless, ageless soul.

Ritual Ceremony:-A specific form of movement, a manipulation of objects or inner processes designed to produce desired effects. In religion ritual is geared toward union with the Divine. In magickal works it produces a specific state of consciousness that allows the magician to move energy toward needed goals.

Ritual Consciousness:-A specific, alternate state of awareness necessary to the successful practice of magick. This state is achieved through the use of visualization and ritual. The conscious mind becomes attuned with the psychic mind, a state in which the magician senses energies, gives them purpose, and releases them toward a specific goal. It is a heightening of senses, an expanded awareness of the nonphysical world, a linking with nature and with Deity.

Ritual Tools:-General name for magickal tools used by a witch or magician. They vary by tradition and usually represent one of the elements.

Runes:-A set of symbols used both in divination and magickal work. There are several types will different origins- Scandinavian, Norse, Germanic.

Sabbat:-A witch's festival.

Scourge:-Small device made from leather or hemp which resembles a whip and is used in flagellation rites within some traditions.

Scrying:-A method of divination. To gaze at or into an object (a quartz crystal sphere, a pool of water, reflections, a candle flame) to still the conscious mind in order to contact the psychic mind. Scrying allows the scryer to become aware of events prior to their actual occurrence, as well as to perceive past or present events through other than the five senses.

Shaman:-A man or woman who has obtained knowledge of the subtler dimensions of the Earth, usually through periods of alternate states of consciousness. Various types of ritual allow the shaman to pierce the veil of the physical world and to experience the realm of energies. This knowledge lends the shaman the power to change his or her world through magick.

Shamanism:-The practice of shamans, usually ritualistic or magickal in nature, sometimes religious.

Shillelagh:-Magickal tool corresponding to the staff in other traditions. Usually made from blackthorn wood.

Sigil:-Magically oriented seal, sign, glyph, or other device used in a magickal working. Ones you create yourself are the most effective. Sigils can be used on letters, packages, clothing, etc.

Simple Feast:-A ritual meal shared with the Goddess and God.

Sky Father:-Shamanistic in origin. It assigns deification to the sky as a male entity.

Skyclad:-The act of celebrating or performing magickal works in the nude. Considered deeply spiritual, NOT sexual.

Solitary:-Pagan who works and worships alone.

Spell:-A magickal ritual, usually non-religious in nature and often accompanied by spoken words. It should be clear, concise, focused and emotional. Need must be present.

Spiral:-Symbol of coming into being.

Staff:-Ritual tool which corresponds to the wand or athame.

Stang:-Ritual tool from Pagan Rome which resembles a two-pronged trident. Often used in place of the wand or circle.

Subconscious Mind:-Part of the mind which functions below the levers we are able to access in the course of a normal working day. This area stores symbolic knowledge, dreams, the most minute details of every experience ever had by a person.

Summerland:-The Pagan Land of the Dead.

Sympathetic Magick:-Concept of likes attract. Most common way spells are worked.

Talisman:-An object charged with personal power to attract a specific force or energy to its bearer.

Tarot Cards:-Set of 78 cards which feature pictures and symbols used to conned the diviner with the collective unconscious.

Tarologist:-One adept at the art and science of handling the Tarot.

Threefold Law:-Karmic principle that energy that is released is returned three times over.

Tradition:-Branch of paganism followed by any individual Pagan or coven.

Trilithon:-A stone arch made from two upright slabs with one lying atop these. They are featured in Stonehenge.

Triple Goddess:-One Goddess in all of her three aspects: Maiden, Mother, Crone.

Virgin:-Youngest aspect of the Triple Goddess. Also know as the Maiden. Represented by the waxing moon, colors white and blue. Her Sabbats are Imbolc and Ostara.

Vision Quest:-Using astral projection, bi-location, or dream time to accomplish a specific goal. Also called path working.

Visualization:-The process of forming mental images. Magickal visualization consists of forming images of needed goals during ritual. It is also used to direct personal power and natural energies for various purposes during magick, including charging and forming of the magick circle.

Wand:-Ritual tool brought to the craft from ritual magick.

Warlock:-Antiquated term misused in reference to a male Witch. It means oath-breaker or Liar. Most Pagans, Witch's find the term offensive.

Web Weaving:-Networking with other magickal people via conversation, writing, e-mail, to gather information which will mutually assist each party.

Wheel of the Year:-One full cycle of the seasonal year.

Wicca:-A modern Pagan religion with spiritual roots in the earliest expressions of reverence for nature. Some major identifying motifs are: reverence for both the Goddess and God; acceptance of reincarnation and magick; ritual observance of astronomical and agricultural phenomena; and the use of magickal circles for ritual purposes.

Wicce:-Synonymous with Wicca. In some circles, Wicce is used for women and Wicca is used for men.

Widdershins:-Counter-clockwise motion, usually used for negative magickal purposes, or for dispersing negative energies or conditions such as disease.

Witch:-A practitioner of folk magick, particularly that kind relating to herbs, stones, colors, wells, rivers, etc. It is used by some Wiccans to describe themselves. This term has nothing to do with Satanism.

Witchcraft:-The craft of the witch- magick, especially magick utilizing personal power in conjunction with the energies within stones, herbs, colors, and other natural objects. This belief system also has nothing to do with Satanism.

Yggdrasil:-One of the best known Tree of Life symbols. It unites all existence from the Underworld, to the Physical world.

www.ingramcontent.com/pod-product-compliance
Lightning Source LLC
Chambersburg PA
CBHW031255280526
45784CB00004B/1862